MEDITERRANEAN SEA

ISRAEL→ Canaan

DEAD SEA

Pyramids of Giza ▲
Memphis ■

Edom

Sinai

Lower Egypt

Midian

Nile River

Amarna ■

Arabian Desert

SAUDI ARABIA

EGYPT

Karnak ◆

Upper Egypt

RED SEA

ERT

Nubian Desert

ETHIOPIA

The GODS and
GODDESSES
of ANCIENT
EGYPT

Seshat

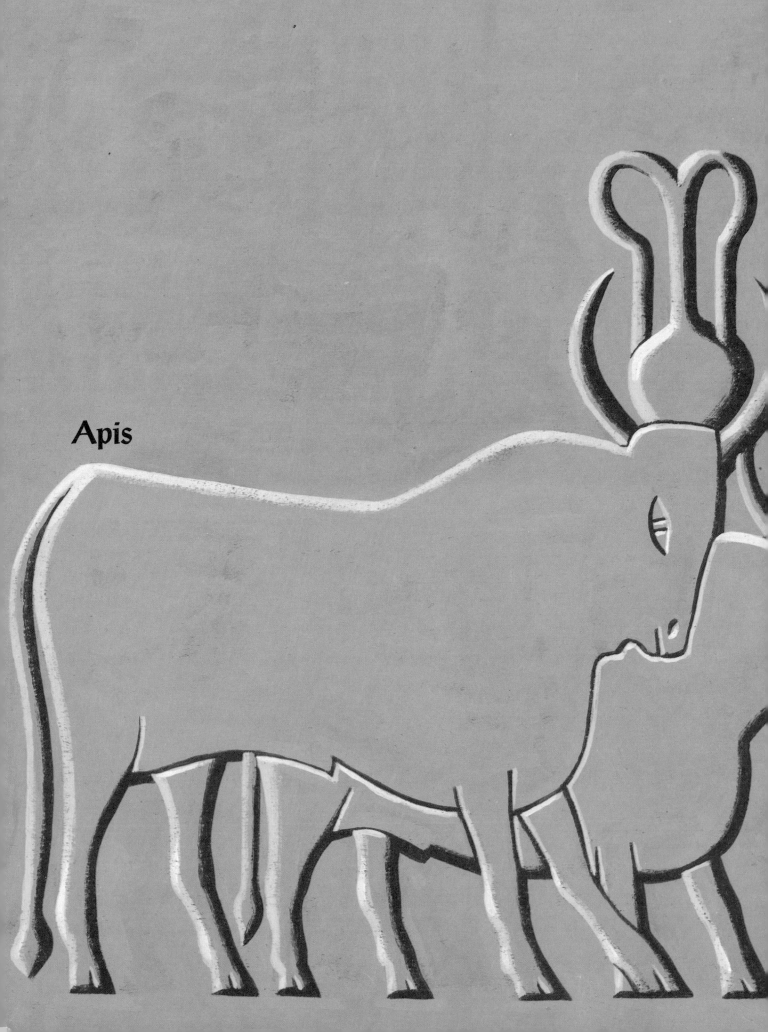

Apis

The GODS and GODDESSES of ANCIENT EGYPT

Leonard Everett Fisher

Holiday House/New York

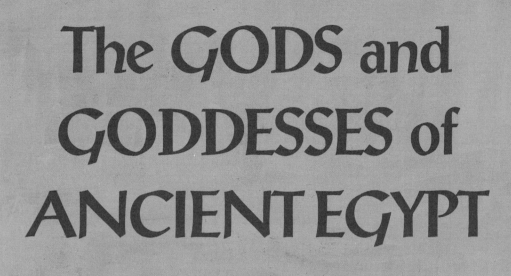

Thoth

Library of Congress Cataloging-in-Publication Data
Fisher, Leonard Everett.
The gods and goddesses of ancient Egypt/Leonard Everett Fisher.
p.   cm.
Includes bibliographical references.
Summary: Relates the history of the gods and goddesses worshipped
by the ancient Egyptians and describes how they were depicted.
ISBN 0-8234-1286-5 (lib.)
1. Gods, Egyptian—Juvenile literature.   2. Goddesses, Egyptian—
Juvenile literature.   3. Mythology, Egyptian—Juvenile literature.
[1. Mythology, Egyptian.]   I. Title.
BL2441.2.F57   1997   96-42068   CIP   AC
299'.31—dc20

INTRODUCTION

The blazing sun inspired awe in the people of Ancient Egypt. In Lower Egypt, the world's longest river, the Nile, emptied into the Mediterranean Sea and made the rainless land fertile. Further south, the people of Upper Egypt also baked under a scorching sun. They huddled close to the Nile, keeping as far away from the sizzling sands of the Sahara Desert as they could.

For nearly 3,500 years, these Ancient Egyptians worshipped the air, wind, and sky; the earth, rain, and water; life, death, and their rulers, the pharaohs, who were thought to be descended from the gods. They worshipped other gods, too, including Seshat, goddess of librarians and writing, who was represented as a woman with a star on her headdress and a pen in her hand; Apis, the bull, a god of lifegiving force; and Thoth, who was sometimes depicted as an ibis, god of the moon, magic, and wisdom.

The Egyptian gods and goddesses were represented by humans and animals, including birds, cats, lions, cows—even crocodiles and baboons. The greatest of all their gods, and the one the Egyptians prayed to most, was Ra, the sun, the supreme god.

RA
God of All Creation

In Lower Egypt, Ra — the sun — was the most powerful god in the universe.

Ra emerged from Nun, the raging waters of chaos. He sailed through the sky in a boat and created everything on earth: water, air, land, plants, all living creatures, and gods. When Ra sailed under the world and disappeared, the coal-black darkness of night followed. But Ra always returned, only to vanish again. There were some who thought that Ra was born a baby every morning, became an adult by noon, and died an old man at night.

Sometimes Ra was shown as a man; sometimes as a man with the head of a falcon. No matter how he was represented, he was always identified by a sun disk — with or without horns.

In Upper Egypt, people worshipped a sun god called Amon. They built a great temple devoted to him on the Nile at Karnak. By 1570 B.C., Amon and Ra had become one in the eyes of all Egyptians. From then on he was called Amon-Ra, or Amon-Re, king of the gods and goddesses.

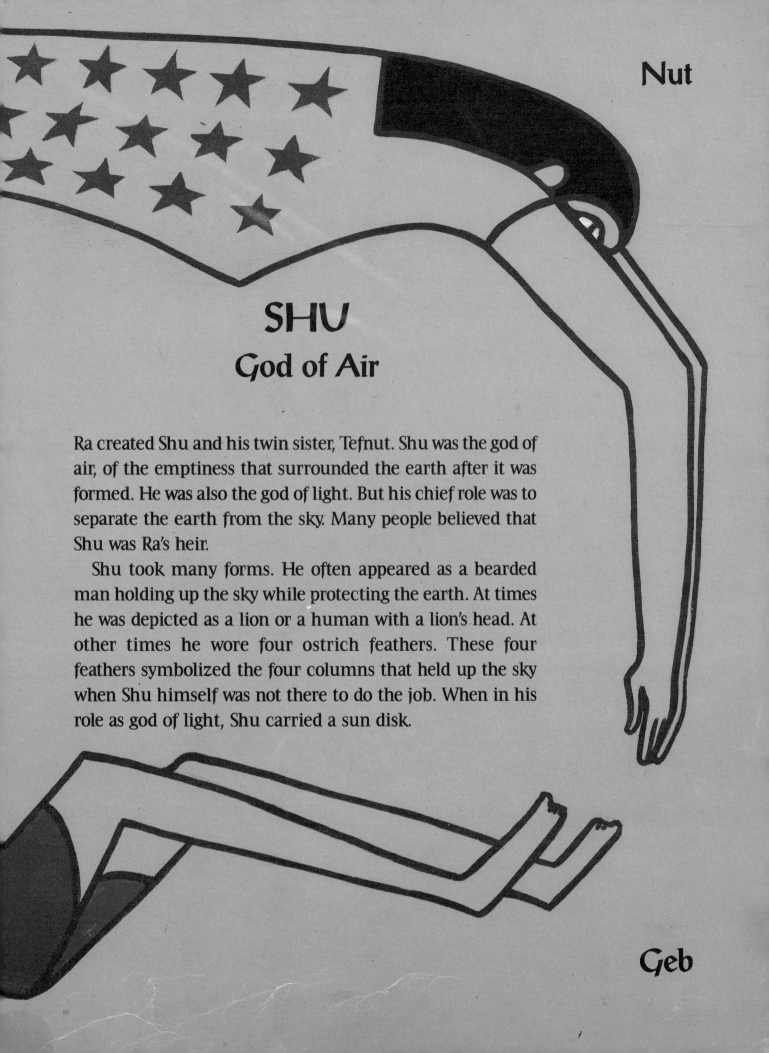

Nut

SHU
God of Air

Ra created Shu and his twin sister, Tefnut. Shu was the god of air, of the emptiness that surrounded the earth after it was formed. He was also the god of light. But his chief role was to separate the earth from the sky. Many people believed that Shu was Ra's heir.

Shu took many forms. He often appeared as a bearded man holding up the sky while protecting the earth. At times he was depicted as a lion or a human with a lion's head. At other times he wore four ostrich feathers. These four feathers symbolized the four columns that held up the sky when Shu himself was not there to do the job. When in his role as god of light, Shu carried a sun disk.

Geb

TEFNUT
Goddess of Morning Dew

Morning dew was considered a divine gift in the relentlessly hot, dry heat of Ancient Egypt. Dew and rain came from the tears of Ra's daughter, Tefnut. Tefnut cried from the terrible strain of helping Shu, her twin brother, hold up the sky. Wherever Tefnut's tears dampened the parched earth, green plants poked through the ground and grew.

Once Tefnut fled from Ra into the desert of Nubia in Upper Egypt, causing a great drought in Lower Egypt. There, in Nubia, she thrived as a lioness. Ra sent Shu disguised as a lion to bring her back and end the drought. After that, Tefnut, wearing her father's sun disk, was often seen as a lioness, or a woman with a lion's head.

GEB
God of the Earth

Shu and Tefnut married and had two children, Geb and Nut. They were born holding each other in an embrace that seemed unbreakable. Ra ordered Shu, his son, to separate the children. When they were separated, Nut became the sky, while Geb became the earth. Shu grew old keeping the sky and earth apart.

Geb was usually shown on his back. His knees were bent and he was propped up by his elbows. His bent knees represented mountains, and the crook of his elbows represented valleys. Sometimes Geb appeared as a goose, or with a goose on his head. In that form, Geb was known as the "the Great Cackler," the fowl that laid the egg out of which came the earth.

NUT
Goddess of the Sky

Nut was most often seen with her body arched over the earth. Only her toes and fingers touched the ground, while her father, Shu, supported the rest of her. There were times, however, that Nut was represented as a sow with suckling piglets. These piglets, which she hid during the day, were the stars. Ancient Egyptians believed that Nut was visiting Geb when night fell. When storms darkened the sky during the day, blocking out the sun, they believed that Nut had fallen.

Nut married her brother, Geb. Together they had four children: Osiris, Isis, Set, and Nephthys. Nut had another daughter, Hathor, with Ra.

OSIRIS
God of the Underworld

Osiris, one of the sons of Nut and Geb, traveled throughout Egypt, teaching the people how to farm and build cities and temples. He civilized Egypt. As god of farming, Osiris assumed many of the powers of his father, Geb, god of the earth.

Osiris married his sister Isis. Later, he was murdered by his jealous brother, Set, and his body was tossed into the Nile. Isis found Osiris's body, and, helped by her sister, Nephthys, Thoth, and others, brought him back to life. Surprisingly, Osiris preferred to leave the cares of the living world and returned to the world of the dead. There he became god of the dead—god of the underworld.

Most Ancient Egyptians saw Osiris in the flooding, receding, and flooding again of the waters of the Nile. The rise and fall of the Nile was tied to Osiris's birth, death, and resurrection.

Osiris was often represented as a mummified pharaoh, sometimes painted green, sometimes black, swathed in white linen wrappings. Like the living pharaoh, he was seen holding the trappings of royal power—the crook, whip, or scepter.

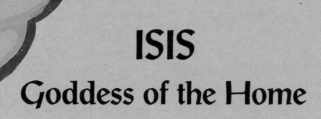

ISIS
Goddess of the Home

One of Nut and Geb's two daughters, Isis was credited for teaching the crafts of spinning, weaving, and other household skills to the women of Ancient Egypt.

Isis married her brother Osiris. After giving birth to their son, Horus, she became a goddess of motherhood. Isis was honored as a faithful, loyal wife and for her love of children, whom she protected against harm and disease. Isis represented what was fertile in Ancient Egypt.

After Set murdered Osiris, Isis was worshipped as a goddess of mourners. She usually appeared with a throne as her headdress, but was sometimes shown wearing either a sun or moon disk bordered by feathers, or a cow's horns. At times, her human head was replaced with that of a cow. In her role as mourner and protector of the dead, Isis wore huge wings.

SET
God of the Desert

If there was one god in Ancient Egypt who represented evil, it was Set. As Isis was the goddess of farm-rich, fertile Egypt, Set was the god of its barren, sun-baked desert. Dissatisfied with ruling only dry Upper Egypt, Set schemed and finally grabbed the more fertile Lower Egypt for himself by murdering his brother, Osiris. He made life miserable for his sisters, Isis and Nephthys, and his nephew, Horus. He even threatened Ra with his mischief. But in the end both Ra and Horus had their revenge for the murder of Osiris. Horus defeated Set in battle and Ra chased him far back into the desert where he ruled as god of nothing more than storm and sand.

To Ancient Egyptians red was the color of evil. And so Set was seen with red, flaming eyes and red hair. Set often appeared as a crocodile, but there were times he was seen as a pig, wild boar, or serpent — even a hippopotamus. Sometimes, Set appeared as a man with the head of a long-snouted monster, which seemed to suit his nature.

NEPHTHYS
Goddess of Mourning

Married to her twin brother Set, Nephthys could find nothing good in him. She wanted children, but Set, the god of the desert where nothing grew, could not have them. Eventually Nephthys left Set. Disguising herself as her sister, Isis, she tricked her brother, Osiris, and bore his child, Anubis. When Osiris was slain, Nephthys helped Isis find his body and bring it back to life. She also told Isis about her baby.

Isis did not feel outraged or betrayed. Instead she blamed Set for all the trouble. Forgiving her sister, Isis adopted Anubis as her own child. Afterwards, Nephthys became a goddess of mourning, a friend and protector of the dead, like her sister, Isis. She always stood at the head of the coffin that would take the deceased to the underworld, with outspread wings.

HORUS
God of Life

Son of Osiris and Isis, and something of a weakling as a child, Horus was constantly at the mercy of his uncle Set. When Osiris traveled around Egypt, Set would send serpents to sting Horus and diseases to kill him. But Isis protected Horus from Set. After Osiris's murder, Horus and Isis fled to the marshes, where they lived on the edge of starvation.

While Horus was growing up, Osiris would emerge from the underworld from time to time to teach him the arts of warfare. Finally, no longer a weakling, but a full grown warrior god, Horus attacked Set to avenge his father's death. After a long series of battles, Horus wounded Set badly, defeated him, and sent him retreating to his desert home which Ra forbade him ever to leave again.

Horus was always represented as a male figure with the head of a falcon whose eyes were the sun and the moon.

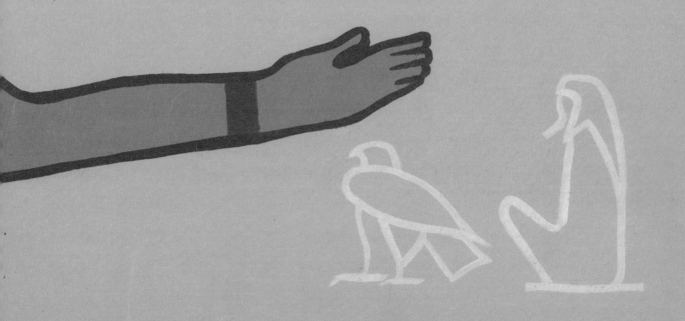

ANUBIS
God of the Dead

Anubis was Osiris's second son and Horus's half brother. He had one very clear duty—he was the undertaker. Anubis's job was to prepare the dead for their journey to eternal life, conduct their funerals, and accompany them to their tombs, where Osiris would greet them. Everything that was done at the funeral of an Ancient Egyptian was done in the name of Anubis.

Anubis was usually represented as a man with the head of a jackal. At times he appeared as a dog, guarding the dead forever.

HATHOR
Goddess of Love

Gentle Hathor, daughter of Ra and Nut, was also a sky goddess. Her concern for humanity—especially the poor—and her interest in love, music, and dance gave her a special place in the hearts of the women of Ancient Egypt. They considered her the guardian of pregnant women. Hathor played a role in funeral ceremonies as well. She was the goddess who provided food and water for the souls of the dead to ease their journeys to the underworld.

Usually, Hathor was depicted as a star-studded cow suckling the dead. Sometimes she appeared as a cow-headed woman offering the bread and water of life, or as a woman with cow's horns flanking a sun disk.

NEKHEBET
Goddess of Royal Protection

The domain of the goddess Nekhebet was the scorching desert of Upper Egypt. Where she originated — who was her mother, who was her father — is not known. Those in Egypt's southern region where Nekhebet was worshipped liked to think that she was a daugther of Ra, and that Hathor, Isis, and Nephthys were her sisters, and Osiris and Set, her brothers — especially Set, whose crimes brought him banishment to the same blazing desert.

Whatever her origins, Nekhebet had both powerful and pleasing aspects. Like Hathor, she was worshipped as a guardian of pregnant women and childbirth. She also protected the bodies of the common poor who were flung unceremoniously into the desert of Upper Egypt after their deaths. Her major job was protector of the pharaoh.

In all these roles, Nekhebet appeared as a vulture, or as a woman with a vulture's head. When protecting the pharaoh, Nekhebet took the form of a vulture whose wings spread over the royal figure, and whose talons held one of the royal symbols such as the pharaoh's ring.

FAMILY TREE

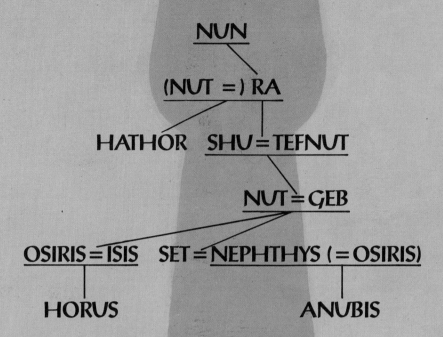

NUN

(NUT =) RA

HATHOR   SHU = TEFNUT

NUT = GEB

OSIRIS = ISIS   SET = NEPHTHYS (= OSIRIS)

HORUS   ANUBIS

PRONUNCIATION GUIDE

Capital letters indicate the stressed syllable.

Seshat	*SESH-it*	Nut	*noot*
Apis	*AYE-pis*	Osiris	*oh-SIGH-ris*
Thoth	*thahth* or *tawte*	Isis	*EYE-sis*
Ra	*rah* or *ray*	Set	*set* or *sate*
Nun	*none*	Nephthys	*NEF-this*
Amon	*AH-men* or *AYE-men*	Horus	*HOR-us*
Shu	*shoo*	Anubis	*a-NEW-bis*
Tefnut	*TEF-noot*	Hathor	*HATH-or*
Geb	*gehb*	Nekhebet	*neck-HEB-it*

BIBLIOGRAPHY

Budge, E.A. Wallis. *Egyptian Language*. New York: Dover Edition, 1978.

Cotterell, Arthur. *A Dictionary of World Mythology*. New York: G.P. Putnam's Sons, 1979.

Desroches-Noblecourt, Christiane. *Tutankhamen*. New York: New York Graphic Society, 1963.

Gardner, Helen. *Art through the Ages*. New York: Harcourt Brace & Co., 1948.

Hart, George. *Ancient Egypt*. New York: Alfred J. Knopf, 1990.

Ions, Veronica. *Egyptian Mythology*. New York: Bedrick Books, 1982.

Leeming, David Adams. *The World of Myths*. New York: Oxford University Press, 1990.

Willis, Roy, ed. *World Mythology*. New York: Henry Holt & Co., 1993.

LIBYA

Libyan Desert

SAHARA DES

1 inch equals approximately 36 miles